BRENT ROBERTS

Unlocking Door to Door Sales

A Beginner's Guide in Door to Door Sales

Contents

1

Intruduction

I had my first experience in sales as a college student in 1996. At that time, I wasn't familiar with selling, or pest control. I heard about a job selling pest control door-to-door, and that the top reps had made over fifty thousand dollars, which sounds almost laughable in today's world for a door-to-door rep, but back then that was good money! What started out as a summer job in 1996 turned into years of subsequent experience with sales, leadership and training, entrepreneurship, and a lifestyle that never would have been possible without taking that leap into the world of sales. Whether you are selling services, products, properties, ideas or lifestyles, everything in the world is driven by sales and those that have mastered the ability to create an exchange of something you have for something you want.

The beauty of sales is that almost all sales jobs pay commission on the number of sales you make, and/or the amount of revenue your sales generate. Sales is the ultimate pay-for-performance job, so take full advantage! You can make as much as you are willing to work for, so give it your best effort! Eat it. Drink it. Sleep it. Keep yourself in a constant mindset of selling. Look for ways to create opportunities for yourself. Wasting time will only limit the amount of money you can make and minimize the amount of experience you gain.

The more effort you put in the more likely you will be successful. Those who have been successful in sales have been so because they dedicated themselves to putting in the time. You will find that if you are consistently spending more time working leads than anyone else, you will be consistently more productive. Commission-based jobs all boil down to how much money you want to make, and the effort you are willing to put forth to reach your goals.

This book is by no means an exhaustive sales manual, I tell my story of getting into door-to-door sales and about fundamentals of how door to door sales can be an effective model for growth, as well as laying out the framework of the attitude and mindset necessary to have success. This book will also touch on the basic elements of a sale; however, it is not meant to be a deep dive. The concepts and ideas presented come from years of experience in selling everything from home services to mortgages. It is important to remember that every person is different in their own personality and selling style, and how you apply these fundamentals will determine what you get out of the material.

2

Getting into Door to Door Sales

I grew up on a family farm in a small town called Weiser (pronounced Weezer) outside of Boise, Idaho. We farmed just under two thousand acres of row crops and raised everything from sugar beets to wheat, onions, corn, and of course, potatoes! We worked hard and I spent the summers doing the typical farm-kid work of changing hand lines, hoeing weeds out of the fields, driving tractors and 10-wheel farm trucks like a boss! We lived right on the Snake River, so our house was always infested with spiders. We had these huge wolf spiders that would build massive webs all over the house and all the outbuildings. One time, when I was in high school, I had one crawl across my mouth while I was sleeping! My family never gave pests much thought. So, when my good friend that was just a year older than me told me that he had sold pest control that summer, I had no clue what he was even talking about. My concept of pest control consisted of mixing two-and-a-half gallon jugs of pesticide into huge tanks on a tractor and then spraying it out in the field. Even after him explaining that they were spraying houses, it still didn't make sense to me. The thing that interested me about the whole idea was that he had made over twenty-five thousand dollars in the summertime, and that's all I cared about!

When I went to college, everyone was talking about what they were going to do to make money. At that time, door to door sales was still somewhat in its infancy. My older brother had sold encyclopedias door to door, but I don't know if he made any money. I assume he didn't because he only did it for one summer. My only criteria for what I wanted to do as a summer job was whatever was going to make the most money. I'm shameless and I didn't really care what I would be doing. My friend told me about a meeting where there would be free pizza and that they would be talking about selling pest control. We showed up to a hotel conference room filled to capacity with other guys that were curious about the job and others that just showed up for the free pizza. The guys that were there to talk about the job were all in fancy suits and ties. They gave a 30-minute pump-up presentation about how awesome the job was and then said that they would be holding interviews, and that they were only hiring a select group. I booked my appointment, waited in line, and interviewed with one of the suit-guys.

The call didn't come until the next day. An office girl called and told me that I didn't make the cut. I didn't care what she said, I was determined to get that job. My friend was one of the top reps the previous year, and I knew he had some pull with the company, so I told him to call them back and get me in! I met back up with the same suit-guy I had met with before and he consented to give me the job but that I would have to be in the same office as my friend, which was great by me!

The rest of that semester before the selling season was peppered with sporadic training and licensing meetings. The company wanted to get everyone licensed in California for the Branch II exam, which is probably the hardest and most intense tests in the country for pest control competence. We all passed the exam and decided that we would go to Albuquerque, New Mexico.

3

That First Summer

There was a basic dress code for selling, which consisted of khaki shorts, which we were responsible for providing, and a polo shirt and hat, which the company would provide. I searched everywhere for khaki shorts and couldn't find any, so I bought a single pair of khaki pants. My roommate was dating a girl that knew how to sew, and I had her cut the pants into shorts and then sew cuffs at the bottom. Laugh all you want; they were as lame as you can imagine – but we all had cuffs in our shorts. I'm sure they probably also had pleats in the front. The hats we were issued were equally lame. They were also a khaki, denim-type fabric with an adjustable fabric strap and a brass buckle in the back – just to put a punctuation mark on our uniform. This was also before cell phones. But halfway through that summer of 1996, there was a major breakthrough in technology, and they came out with pagers that we didn't know how to use, but we wore them because we believed they made us look more official.

In Albuquerque, we had 16 reps in our office: 14 guys and 2 girls; plus a manager and his wife. Our apartment complex had a swimming pool and a hot tub and as young college kids in the late 90's we all felt like we had really arrived in life. All of us were super ambitious about having a successful summer.

Our day consisted of making calls from 10 to 11 in the morning to leads we would generate during the day throughout the summer; then we had correlation from 11-12 and then head out to our areas to knock until dark and then come home and work the phones again until our call-sheets were exhausted. The schedule that summer was grueling and intense but manageable. We were all a long way from home, so there wasn't anything else to do but work, so most of us did. We would always show up about an hour early for correlation. Our manager had two folding-tables set up in the small living room of his apartment with several phones on each table. We would use these phones to make call-backs. It seems like we always had plenty of contacts to call before correlation, and it created a competitive environment having more reps than there were phones. Correlation was always super organized, and the marketing company we worked for had reps all across the country, so we would get daily updates on the top reps in the company and could see how our office was stacking up. After correlation, we would head out to our areas to sell. There were no navigation systems, so we all just had the big fold-up Rand McNally maps. The passenger in the car would take up all of their side, and into the driver's side of the car with their mess of map which was folded out to be able to help navigate the driver. Some navigators were better than others and could direct the driver without rotating the map upside-down every time a turn was made, but others would constantly have to rotate their map-mess.

Once we got out to where we would be knocking, we were committed to being stranded in that area. We would sometimes take a quick break for lunch, but many times we would just bring a cleaned-out milk jug full of frozen water and we would drink it throughout the day as it melted. For food, we would sometimes just bring power-bars, but other times we would just grab whatever was the quickest. Even then, we understood that time was money; and we didn't want to waste any more time than was absolutely necessary. This included bathroom breaks. Bathroom use was always sketchy because we were stranded in subdivisions, so it was either humiliate yourself and ask a customer, or find an alternative option using your imagination.

That first summer in Albuquerque, we had stopped to eat at a greasy burger dive on the outskirts of town next to a lower-income area that we knew was full of roaches. After lunch, my friend dropped me off and drove his car to the other side of the area. I had been knocking for about half an hour when my stomach started disapproving of the tasty burger and fries I had for lunch. My focus turned from making sales, to finding the right person who I would feel comfortable enough to ask to use their bathroom. I didn't have options, and I was running out of time, and so the next person that answered the door would have to do. I knocked and a middle-aged Hispanic woman opened the door. I started my spiel, but she quickly let me know that she didn't speak English. Luckily, I had served a mission in Chile and was fluent in Spanish, so I asked if I could please use her bathroom. She reluctantly invited me in, showed me the bathroom door and went back to visiting with her friend that was sitting on the couch. The house was probably a thousand square feet, so the bathroom door was connected to the living room where the lady and her friend were talking. I was desperate, so I quickly went in, locked the door, threw down my khaki shorts, sat down and started making a mess. I lost all sense of dignity. I could hear the women talking as they were sitting on the couch, so I knew they could hear the entire episode I was having. The bathroom door had a two-inch gap between the floor, so there was hardly anything to break the sounds. And once you start, there's no stopping, *and* it's not like I wanted to leave before I felt confident that I had vacated everything from my bowels that wanted out. I was in trouble, and I knew it. I finished up, made sure I left the bathroom as I had found it, and had my tail between my legs as I opened the bathroom door to see the two women looking at me in disgust. I didn't know what to do, so I just put my hat in my hands, said, "Lo siento" and walked out the front door.

I was working for what was then, the world's largest pest control company. They were the bulwark of the industry and that year they had come up with a patented Wall Injection System, which consisted of hollow plastic plugs with an attached plastic cap, that could be inserted into a hole that was drilled into the drywall. The technicians would install these plugs and would thereby be able to insert a tube from an aerosol-can, so the inside of the wall void could be treated. The entire service consisted of this treatment on the inside of the home under the sinks, and then a meager treatment with a pump-it-up spray can on the outside of the house. This service was done for just $25 per month with a 12-month commitment. Those were different days for sure.

The technicians we had were their own breed as well. They had a guy working for them who was a hard-core pest guy. He carried his sprayer like a Colt 45, and he was the sheriff of his pest control world. He showed up to do a service I had sold, and me and the gal I had signed up met him at the curb and showed him the water meter where large oriental roaches congregated. He lit up a cigarette and went back to his truck to get his sprayer. Once he had mixed his potion, he came back to the water meter where we were, set his spray can on the grass and with the spray wand in one hand and his cigarette in the other, he proceeded to saturate the water meter. Roaches scurried to get away from the spray, but they couldn't get away from his boot. He made sure as he stepped on them that they knew they had messed with the wrong technician that day as he smeared their carcasses into the grass. Fortunately for me, the lady I had sold was equally enthused and encouraged him with chants of, "Get 'em"!

Our sales team was a hodge-podge of personalities. Some were harder workers than others, but everyone still had success. Along with no cell phones and all the other technologies that were invented years later, there was also no such thing as earbuds, or any kind of music other than a Walkman, or whatever you could find at Radio Shack. We had this one-pond duck in our office that bought an analog hand-held transistor radio (Google it) and a set of foam-padded headphones so he could listen to the radio in between doors. He knocked doors the rest of the summer with that radio clipped to his belt. He would leave his headphones on until a customer came to the door, and then, he would use the manual volume dial to turn his radio down and proceed with his spiel. The best part is that his radio wasn't waterproof, and not that this scene needed any additional comedic help, but whenever rain was in the forecast, he would put his radio inside a bread sack! There he was, walking down the street with his headphones on, and a bread sack clipped to his belt! The guy still made sales as awkward as he was; and he was a super hard worker.

We ended up adding over four thousand accounts to the two Albu-querque branches we covered between the sixteen original reps, plus a few more that came towards the end of the summer. It was way more than the branch manager had anticipated, so it ended up being somewhat of cluster for them; but selling that summer changed my life and the lives of all of us that had success. I ended up selling 325 accounts that first summer and made just over twenty-three thousand dollars. I was ruined and hooked. I could never go back to working a wage job again. Once you find something that will pay based on effort versus everyone getting paid the same regardless of input, you can never go back. At least I couldn't.

4

Growing Your Service Business with Door Sales

There is not another method of putting on accounts that is as targeted and predictable as door-to-door sales. There are companies that will do all the recruiting, hiring, training, payroll and housing of sales teams all across the country. So if you are looking at having a door team, you don't have to recruit and train sales guys and figure out where they're going to stay during the summer, or make sure they have furniture, or do any of those things. You can be as involved, or disengaged as you care to be. You will pay a premium if you subcontract the entire process, but the model still works. Most companies that subcontract out salespeople are going to charge anywhere from 85% to above 100% of annual contract value. It's not cheap, so you better have your pencil sharpened and make sure you have enough cash or credit to float you through until those accounts are paid for. But being able to add a couple thousand, or way more, recurring customers to your business in four to six months is a game-changer for anyone looking to grow their business rapidly.

The alternative to door salesmen is just to do what you and everyone else has always done. Sure, you can pour money into your online campaigns, or do geo-targeted mailers, or billboards, or email campaigns, or any of the other tried and tested methods for growth. But how many total customers you get from those campaigns, and how many customers you get from each area is going to be an educated estimate/guess at best; and regardless of whether you get any sales or not from that campaign, the price is static; and most of the time, you pay for the campaign up front. There are some up-front costs of a door team, but the real costs are amortized as the sales come in, so at least you can have a better idea of how much growth to expect. And, by the end of the first month, most companies will be able to project how many sales their team is going to put on for you based on historical data, and not just a guess. Their projection should be close, within a reasonable margin for error.

5

The Mental Aspect

S elling is a mindset. Plain and simple. And those who have success in the sales world are those who go out and make things happen. They don't just scavenge for scraps of low-lying fruit. The most successful salespeople are always in the mode of closing deals and making strategic contacts that they know will produce. They don't just sit back and wait for warm leads to come in; but they get out and drive leads.

Just because you aren't outgoing or extroverted doesn't necessarily mean that you can't be successful in sales. Look, there are lots of personalities in the world. I've met plenty of people that are social introverts that killed it at sales. However, I have never known of anyone having success in sales if they weren't minimally competitive. And for me, the scrappier a person is, the better. I've seen people come in with the quintessential necklace and matching gold bracelet they've been wearing since high school, get their butts kicked in sales by the unassuming rep that had something to prove to the world.

Have confidence! Believe you are the best!! Believe you are good enough to sell anyone. Your confidence is demonstrated in the way you present yourself, eye contact, poise, and tone of voice. By convincing yourself that there is no one you cannot sell, your confidence and purpose will be clear to those you communicate with. Positive attitude has everything to do with those you surround yourself with. Lack of confidence can kill your potential as a salesperson. Surround yourself with others who are confident and optimistic. Don't waste your time with pessimists. Their negative influence will have a detrimental effect on your ability to sell. Potential customers know when a salesperson has passion for what they are selling. They can sense when you are confident in your product and when you have doubts. A positive attitude breeds confidence and success. One of the biggest challenges you will face in sales is dealing with rejection. Not everyone you talk to will agree to buy what you are selling, in fact, many will be short-tempered or impatient. Don't let the rejection get you down. Remember, each lead is a brand-new opportunity, so if you are frustrated by the way someone treated you, let it go and move on.

Consumers prefer to buy from someone who can make them feel confident about their decision to make a purchase. Be witty. Think on your feet. Handle objections with a smile. When customers have an objection, don't look at is a negative. Objections are just opportunities to provide more of the awesome features of the product or service you are selling! Be prepared to respond intelligently to every possible concern. You are the expert! Act like it! Always respond to objections and concerns in a positive fashion. The better your ability to handle objections, the more confidence the customer will have in making a purchase from you. If customers have serious concerns, they expect to get serious answers. The more you can help them feel that you are a professional who knows the product and the competition, the easier your job will be.

As the salesperson, YOU need to be sold on what you are selling! Believe in your product. Become an expert! Learn everything there is to know about what you are selling and how it compares to the competition. Learn all the benefits. Know all the features. When you talk about your product, get excited! There is nothing worse than listening to a sales rep trying to sell something they obviously don't believe in. After listening to you, the customer should feel like they can't live without whatever-it-is-you're-selling! Get them on the bandwagon! No one wants to feel like they are missing out; and your job as a salesperson is to create that sense of urgency.

Be creative. You will find that the same concerns and objections will be repeated over and over, day after day. It is important, therefore, to try new ways to resolve the common concerns you hear. No one method will be successful in every situation. That is why practicing and becoming a master at each method will prove to be an important part of your sales technique. When you are in between leads, you can maximize your time by thinking of things you said right and things you said wrong in your last spiel or presentation. When you make a sale, try to think back on what you said that made the customer want to buy from you. If you lose a sale, try to identify where the sale was lost, and then make improvements. Often, you can gain or lose a sale simply by the way you said something, so be conscientious not only of what you say, but how you say things.

Every day of selling is part of your continuing sales education. This is a time to be your own teacher and critic. If you can look at failure as a steppingstone to your next success, then you are on your way to becoming an exceptional salesperson. In the season that Babe Ruth hit the most home runs (60), he was also the player to have the most strikeouts (89). Swing for the fences! There is nothing wrong with going for a home run at every at-bat. That is basically what you are trying to do when you go out selling. Be mindful of the things that are bringing you success and causing failures.

Continue to refine your presentation. Changing things up on a regular basis will keep you sharp and on your toes. Personalize each approach to the customer you are working with. Fluctuate the tone and pitch of your voice. If you sound like a broken record, it will be easy for the customer to tune you out. Try new approaches. It is easy to go into salesman-autopilot. This happens when you have said the same thing over and over again so many times that it becomes impulsive. The more varying approaches you can master, the better you will be able to customize to a wider range of customers. Customize to the customer in every aspect of the sale – in your initial approach, the way you resolve concerns, the features you focus on, and the way you close.

Diversify your personality. This does not mean that you need to create some pseudo personality, or your entire selling style for that matter. Some people are super outgoing, while others are more reserved and introverted. Just because you are somewhat reserved doesn't mean you can't have success at sales. Remember, your competence as a salesperson has more to do with how competitive you are than any other personality trait. Diversifying your personality is about being relatable and genuine. The imperative is to learn how to relate to every type of person by diversifying yourself.

Understanding communication is a fundamental component of successful selling and it is important to understand how to communicate, both in the things you say (verbal), and in the things you don't say (nonverbal). All of this is important because you have to connect with the buyer. Sales communication involves using verbal and nonverbal methods to persuade a consumer to buy a product or service. The sales communication process starts with explaining the important details about whatever it is you are selling, then listening to the customer's opinions and possibly doubts, and then resolving those questions or concerns. Learning how to effectively communicate will dramatically improve your ability to create a need, build rapport, establish value, gain trust, and close deals. Paying attention to the customer's mannerisms will help you weed out non-buyers. Pay attention to body language and be sure you are expressing positive body language.

It is crucial that the customer's first impression of you is a good one. That first impression has less to do with what you say, and more to do with how you appear while you're saying it. Your presence on the doorstep is the first thing that people will notice about you. A happy countenance is the most critical nonverbal cue you can communicate. Smiling and being dressed professionally can bring a customer's guard down. Be relaxed. The way you present yourself says a lot about who you are.

One of my favorite stories is from a good friend that used to work for me. He was the best pure salesman I have ever met. His background was in car sales, but the guy could sell anything, and he was always selling. He would tell you about every piece of clothing he had on, and you would think, "I didn't even know I needed a jacket, but I better get the one he has!". He told me a story one time that when he was selling cars, he sold a brand-new car to a lady, and after the deal was done, she told him that she was just on her way to the grocery store and wasn't even in the market for a new car! He was an excellent communicator, and he had mastered the skills of both verbal and non-verbal communication.

Be sure to attend training meetings! Trainings are a great way to keep you sharp and on top of the latest techniques being practiced in the business. Glean successes from other successful salespeople, and don't discredit a successful tactic even if it comes from an inexperienced salesperson. Over the years, I have learned plenty from reps with very little experience. Be an active participant in the role plays and other activities in training meetings. If someone is having more success than you are, find out why! What are they saying? What type of areas do they target? Do they have any visual aids they are using? What is their work schedule? How are they generating leads? How are they resolving concerns? Find out how they are having success resolving the concerns you are having problems with, and then implement those strategies in your own presentation. Never become so complacent with your sales skills that you think you have learned everything there is to learn about selling. Selling is a massive skillset. Learning as much as possible will help you not only in your current position but in many other aspects of life. Be attentive to things other reps are doing to have success, and don't be afraid to try a technique that is creating sales for another rep, even if it is something that steps totally out of your personality style or comfort zone.

Along with mental toughness, you want to be physically disciplined. Create a routine for success. Get a full night's rest; get up early in the morning; eat a healthy breakfast; get a workout in during your day. If you have any sort of sales training in the mornings, arrive early and be prepared to learn. Take notes, ask questions, be prepared to try the new things you learn about. Don't allow your sales skills to become stagnant. The more you develop your presentation the more polished you will be. Success in sales begins long before you start contacting potential customers. You need a plan! At the beginning of the year, set your yearly goal. Break that goal down into how many sales you need to get each month to achieve your yearly goal. Then set weekly goals for how many sales you need to get to hit your monthly goals. Before you start your week, set a goal of how many sales you want to make, whether that is in quantity of sales, or a cumulative dollar amount, and have that number written down in a place you will see it every morning.

6

The Sales Process

W hen I first started selling, we were trained to have this huge spiel and to just keep talking and never give the customer time to respond because they might say no before we had a chance to tell them about the discount. We had success, of course, and if that is the selling style that works for you then you should keep doing it. But I have had substantially more success when I quickly identify real potential buyers and weed everyone else out. This process also helps keep things in perspective while you are working because if someone is short with you, instead of getting upset, you should actually be grateful, because they just saved you from wasting time with them. You *should* tell them thanks!

Regardless of whether you are trying to make sales, or simply generate leads, and regardless of what you are selling, on any full day of working you can anticipate that only a small percentage of the cold calls you make will actually talk with you. When I am training, I tell reps to plan on between 5-20 people per day. This isn't unique to any specific product or service. I have done door sales all over the country and have found that the number of people that will engage is very similar.

There may be more people that actually buy your product or service depending on your price point, but the number of people that engage is similar regardless of what you are selling. Those that respond and engage are your potential buyers! Focus your time on them! As you get better at sales, you will find that you are able to get more people to engage with you than a newer rep, so you might be more on the side of 10-20 and a newer rep will say that only 5-10 people talked to them. But the point is, your initial spiel should be razor sharp, and all you care about is identifying if this is a person you are going to invest time in, or not. I don't typically spend more than a minute talking with customers that won't engage. It is important when you are giving your spiel at the door that you look for the customer's reaction and are ready to respond to any objections they might have. Use their concerns to your advantage. Play on the hot buttons they bring up.

Let's dive into the spiel. Whether you are out knocking, or working the phones, your spiel is simply what you say in the initial 30 seconds. Create a sense of urgency! Get the customer's attention! Remember, that as a salesperson, you are an intruder to the customer's time. What you say in the first 30 seconds will determine whether that customer will have any interest in lending their attention. Don't talk too fast but get to the point. Time wasted with a non-buyer is money out of your pocket. As you gain experience as a salesperson you will become a master at identifying real buyers and those you are wasting your time with.

Your spiel involves three components:

1. Who you represent.

- Some reps think it is important to say their name along with who they represent. Listen, as awesome as you are, no one cares what your name is when you are cold calling. You can tell them your name after they have engaged with you if you think it's important at that point. Time is money, and all you should care about is determining, as fast as you can, if this person is a worthwhile investment for you. The first two sentences out of my mouth are, "Hey, I just stopped by real quick. I'm with 'such and such company'. Or, if I'm making cold calls on the phone, "Hey, I'm just reaching out really quick. I'm with 'this or that company.'"

2. What problem you are solving – why you are there.

- In pest control I would usually just say, "A lot of what your neighbors have been seeing is _____" (whatever you have been noticing), or "We've been getting a lot of calls out here for ants..." or "You know the Johnson's down the street, right? Their biggest issue has been all the wasps...". Or any variation. Or customize this to make it your own.

If I'm selling solar, I would say, "Everybody out here hates how their power bill is always higher than it should be" or "We've been doing lots of installs out here 'cause everyone is sick of paying the power company" or "People are super sick of the power company always raising their rates".

If you are selling something else, like alarms, or whatever it is, just create one or two sentences that establish the "why" of why you are there; or what problem you are solving.

3. A question to see if this is one of the "five to twenty". This is your Qualifying Question.

- Never ask a yes or no question. This is a leading question to get them engaged, or at a minimum, to gauge their interest level.

For pest control: "What are you seeing the most of?" or "Where have you noticed the most activity?" or "What do you typically do for pest control?" or "Who do you guys use for pest control?" Or create your own, or any variation of any of these.

For solar: "I assume you've thought about solar like everybody else. What's been your biggest hang up?" or "When was the last time you looked into solar?" or "Today, I'm just going through what a general layout would look like based on your roofing configuration. I have some time I could show you that right now, or I could come back this afternoon and go through that with you. What works best for you?"

If you are selling something else, you still get the idea. You probably already have things you have said in the past. Again, all you are doing is trying to determine if they will engage. I always try a few times to get some level of engagement, even if the short spiel doesn't get them going. When you are an experienced salesperson, there is a good chance you can close a deal if someone will just let you talk to them. But if someone won't engage, even at a minimal level, then you just saved yourself a lot of time and you can just move on to the next contact. Never forget, though, that it is equally important to identify those who *would* potentially sign up with the right hot button. You are in charge of your own sales, so make sure you spend all the time necessary with anyone you feel you should.

Once you get through the initial spiel and you have an engaged customer, present the product. This is your opportunity to promote your service, build value, and create a sense of urgency. When you are talking about your product, be enthusiastic! At this point, the customer still isn't excited that you are standing on their doorstep. When you start talking about your service you need to make sure that you do everything you can to raise the customer's interest level and to clearly establish the value your service or product can provide.

Every industry is different, so I don't want to dilute the sales process by going through every possible scenario because some sales are very complex, and some are very simple. Every sale is different, but the main components are all basically the same:

Introduction, What problem you solve - why you are there, Your qualifying question;
    Build value, close;
    Resolve concerns, build value, close;
    Create a sense of urgency, close;
    Resolve concern, build more value, close;
    Resolve concern, close;
    Resolve concern, close.

Continue this process until they sign up or at least give you their phone number. After your initial approach, you are almost always going to be presented with your first objection. Almost no one answers the door saying, "Hey, we've been thinking about getting your service; I was just about to call you!". How you handle objections will determine the progress of the sale, so just absorb, and embrace them! My favorite is when a customer asks if we take care of something specific, or if they ask what we do about a specific issue. As soon as a customer asks a question like that, my response is always, "Let's go take a look at that and I'll give you some options." Take any opportunity you can to get the customer off their doorstep. Your chances of closing a deal are exponentially higher if you can get them off the door. Many times, the first objection is the hardest to overcome, so if you've done it correctly and you have a customer engaged and off their doorstep the rest of the sale is all downhill. After overcoming the first objection, you will begin a pattern of pitching, closing, and overcoming new objections. You may need to repeat this process many times before you get the sale, but each objection you get past will bring you that much closer to the sale.

When working with objections, don't just vomit everything you know on top of the customer. Just resolve the concern or answer the question, tell them something else awesome about your program and give another close. Don't use all the arrows in your quiver. Many first year sales reps feel like they need to tell the customer everything they have ever learned about the service. Just say enough to pique the customer's interest. If a customer asks a question, get to the point. Don't say anything that is going to create more doubt.

The first close, although successful many times, is more just to get the customer to engage. Often, closing will bring concerns immediately out into the open so that you can get to work resolving them. There are many different ways to close a sale. Some are more aggressive than others. This is another area where, as the salesperson, you will have to make the call on the ones that work best for you. This is also an area where it is important to customize to the customer and the situation at hand.

As a salesperson, you should be fearless. You should never be afraid to answer a question or close a deal. Every time you resolve a concern, you should look at it as an opportunity to close the sale. Even if the customer doesn't accept after your first attempt, closing only puts you one step closer to the sale. Don't give up! If you give up the first time a customer says "NO," your success rate is going to end up being very low. Every time a customer says "No" find out what their concerns are, resolve them, and try closing again. Your sales will have a direct relation to how many times you close. Keep in mind, this is going to have to be a good judgment call on your part as the salesman. Obviously, if a person is adamant, just move on.

Rarely will you make a sale without any concerns. When concerns are brought up, they must be received as if you have heard and resolved them a million times. Customers like to test your knowledge to see if you know what you are talking about. Be prepared for all types of questions and concerns. Preparation will come through experience on the doors and by drawing from the experience of other salespeople. Customers will sometimes ask you a question which to them is a serious concern, but to you, it might seem trivial. Regardless of the question, always make the customer feel that their genuine concerns are appreciated. No one likes a salesperson that makes them feel like their questions are stupid. As the salesperson, *you* are the professional. Help the customer feel like they are talking to one. Receiving objections is part of the game. Keep in mind that objections are nothing more than a request for more information. Never view them as anything more. Don't take them personal. Make notes of the successful responses you, or other reps, are saying to resolve concerns.

Whether or not you are making lots of sales on the doors, a big part of your cumulative success is increasing your leads pool. I always try to have a success on every door. I try as hard as I can to get the sale. If I can't get the sale, I try to get a phone number. Going back to the

5-20 rule, I try to get at least a phone number from every single person that engages with me. If I make ten sales in a day, I also want to get ten phone numbers. If I make five sales in a day, I'm shooting for 15 phone numbers. If I can't get a phone number, I commit them to keeping my card, and I tell them to put it in their drawer that has the screwdriver and scissors in it. Everyone has that drawer, and if you didn't make the sale, at a minimum - that's where you want your card! Eventually most people are going to come around and find a need for what you were selling, and you want to maximize your chances for future sales. In every office I ever sold in, I always had more call ins than everyone in the office, and by a large margin.

Have the attitude that you are going to get something from every customer that talks to you. And then, spend time every morning and every evening working that phone list that you have created. As your list of phone numbers grows you will increase the database from which you can generate sales. Be meticulous about making notes about your contacts. The more you remember about a contact the more receptive they will be when you call them back. Write down the best time to contact them, what type of concerns they had, what price you quoted them. You can also make notes to remind you of the person themselves; something you think will jog your memory as to who they are. If you encounter customers who are under contract with other services, get their information – what company they are with, how much they are paying, when their contract expires, and then contact them when that time arrives. By filling your calendar with these contacts, you will build a steady pool of warm leads that will continue to produce for you.

Time can and should be spent calling customers back who have expressed interest. When doing call-backs, get right to the point. Most people on your call-back sheet have already made a decision. Or if they haven't, there are only one or two concerns holding them back. Use the same techniques on the phones as you have developed on the doors. Find out what their concerns are, resolve them, and close the deal.

7

Conclusion

As I stated at the beginning of this book, this is by no means an exhaustive piece. My intention was to create a brief, and hopefully entertaining overview of the things I thought were most important in sales that anyone would be able to breeze through it in a quick sit down. Sales is the most demanding, competitive, and rewarding career path that anyone could possibly embark on. And door to door sales takes grueling to the next level. Those who have the determination to have success at door sales will be successful at whatever they do in life. That's a guarantee! But regardless of whether you bought this book out of curiosity, or you were looking for some motivation, or you're just a sponge and like to soak up anything and everything that has to do with sales, I hope you have enjoyed reading, or listening! I wish you all the luck in the world!

If you found this book helpful, I'd be very appreciative if you left a favorable review for the book on Amazon!